Teaching with
Robert Munsch Books Vol. 2

Amy von Heyking
and
Janet McConaghy

Scholastic Canada Ltd.
Toronto New York London Auckland Sydney
Mexico City New Delhi Hong Kong Buenos Aires

We thank the students who generously shared their work,
and the parents who kindly shared their children's photographs.

Cover and interior design by Andrea Casault
Cover and interior illustrations copyright © by Michael Martchenko
Photo on page 6 by Barry Johnston

Every effort has been made to obtain permission for,
and to credit appropriately, all photographs used in this book.
Any further information will be appreciated and
acknowledged in subsequent editions.

Library and Archives Canada Cataloguing in Publication
Von Heyking, Amy J. (Amy Jeanette), 1965-
Teaching with Robert Munsch books / Amy von Heyking,
Janet McConaghy.

ISBN 0-439-97433-X (v. 1).-ISBN 0-439-95702-8 (v. 2)

1. Munsch, Robert N., 1945- —Study and teaching (Elementary)
2. English language—Study and teaching (Elementary) 3. Language arts
(Elementary) 4. Children's stories, Canadian (English)—Study and teaching
(Elementary) I. McConaghy, Janet II. Title.

PS8576.U575Z92 2003   C813'.54   C2003-901055-4

ISBN-13 978-0-439-95702-1

6 5 4 3 2   Printed in Canada 119   11 12 13 14

Table of Contents

The Story of Robert Munsch

Who is Robert Munsch? He's one of North America's best-loved storytellers, and his books, including the best-selling *Love You Forever*, have been entertaining children for decades.

Robert grew up in a family of nine kids. You might think that would be pretty hard, but he says it was a good thing. He could do the things he liked — like reading — without much interruption. When Robert was younger, he was a "reading freak" and would read anything he could. His favourite book was *The Five Hundred Hats of Bartholomew Cubbins* by Dr. Seuss. He also liked to write poems — funny ones, of course.

It might be hard to believe, but Robert wasn't always a writer. He was working at a daycare centre when his boss's wife, a children's librarian, heard him telling stories. She thought the stories were very good, and told him he should write them down and send them to a publisher.

Can you imagine: nine publishers turned down his stories! Finally one publisher said yes, and that very first Robert Munsch book, *Mud Puddle*, came out in 1979. Even so, it was another five years before Robert finally quit his job at the daycare centre. Since then he has published more than forty books!

Where does Robert get his ideas? They almost always come from kids. Sometimes he'll see someone in the audience when he is doing a storytelling and ask if they would like to be a character in one of the stories. Other times, he'll be inspired by a kid he meets or by a letter someone sends to him. Just about anything can give him an idea. But not all of his stories become books — there are just too many! When he does a storytelling session, he might tell fourteen or fifteen stories, most of them new. But sometimes one story seems stronger than the rest, so he'll take that one and tell it over and over again — sometimes for years. And one day he might decide that the story is ready to become a book.

It's important to Robert that his books can be enjoyed by kids regardless of where they live in North America, or even the world. So if a story is set in Toronto, he wants kids in the Northwest Territories to enjoy it just as much as ones who live in the city, and vice versa. It can be a real trick to get the stories to work out so kids everywhere can relate to them.

Robert likes telling stories in schools and libraries. Sometimes, if he's going to be in a particular area, he'll check to see if a local school has written to him. Then he'll pay them a surprise visit. Sometimes he'll call a library or school and ask them to find an interesting family that he can stay with when he is travelling. Lucky them!

What does Robert do for fun? He likes to read, take his dogs for walks outside of town, ride his bicycle and even climb trees! And he loves to eat "hot, hot chicken wings."

Robert has three children, Julie, Andrew and Tyya, and he's written stories for all of them. The family in *Andrew's Loose Tooth* is Robert Munsch's — or Michael Martchenko's version of them, anyway.

Robert also keeps busy by reading and responding to the letters he gets. Each month he gets about 200 letters from schools and another 200 from individual children. That's a lot of reading and writing to catch up on!

Being a good storyteller is something that Robert has been blessed with. Still, it took him a long time to realize that he was pretty good at it. He often wonders exactly what it is that makes a person a great storyteller. Being able to think on your feet is part of it, but it's also really important to be a good listener — especially when it comes to listening to children. Of course, he's so good at telling stories that it's made him popular with children the world over.

Being a writer takes dedication as well as talent, but as Robert says, "This is the best job I've ever had."

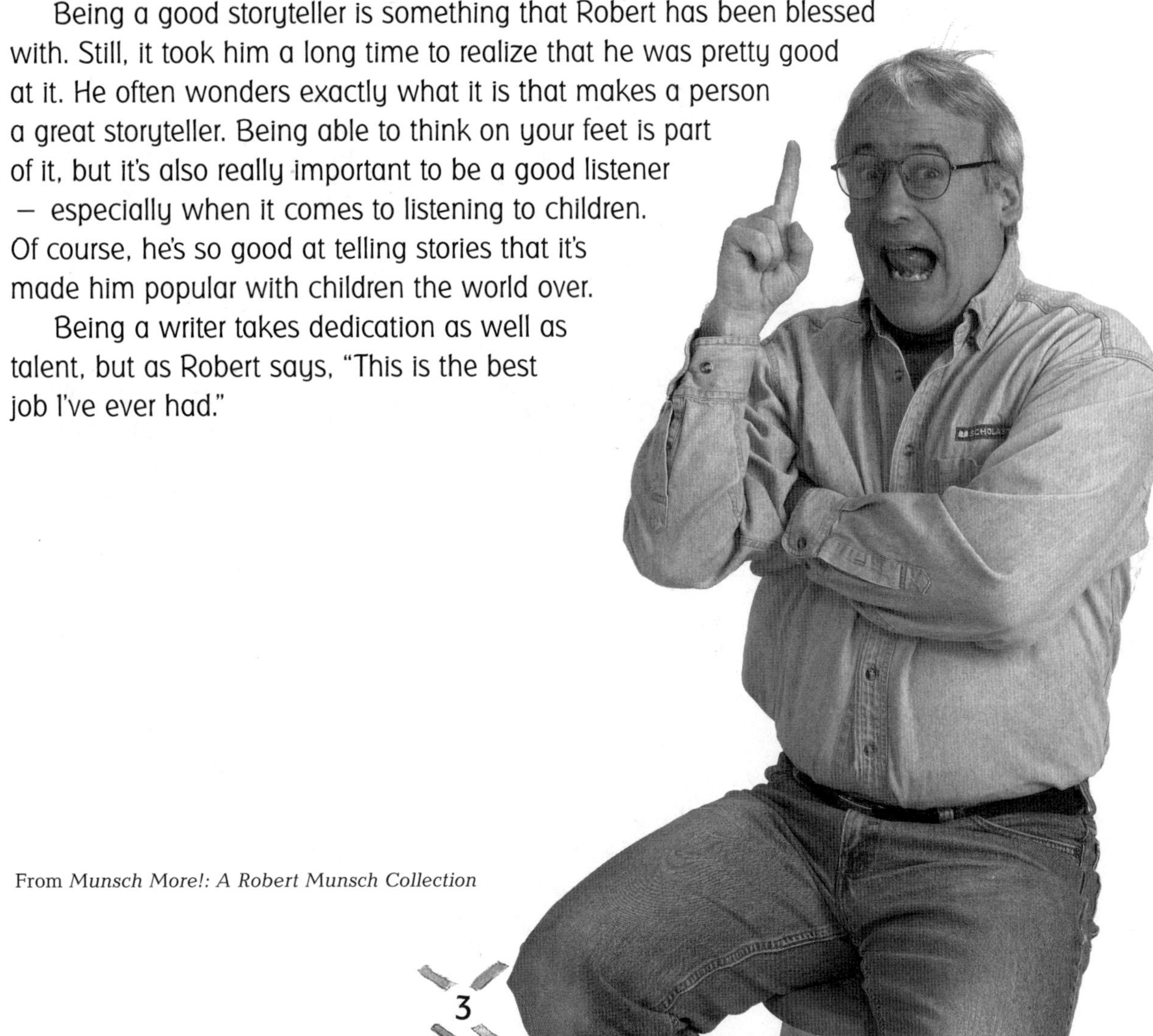

From *Munsch More!: A Robert Munsch Collection*

Robert Munsch Q & A

Q: "Where do you get your ideas? How do you choose which ones to use?"
Katrina, 10 years old

A: "I get my ideas from . . . kids."
("Can you make a story about my ponytail?" – *Stephanie's Ponytail*)

. . . looking at kids." ("Wow! That kid is colouring her fingernails purple!" – *Purple, Green and Yellow*)

. . . visiting families." ("It's my birthday and you're telling stories." – *Moira's Birthday*)

. . . letters." ("When I get Amy out of bed she falls asleep on the floor." – *Get Out of Bed!*)

. . . storytelling." ("I'm going to make up a new story. Who wants to be in it?")

Q: "Are your stories true?"
Duncan, 10 years old

A: "Except for *From Far Away*, my stories are not true. The kids in the stories are real, but the stories are made up."

Q: "Can you write scary stories?"
Linda, 8 years old

A: "I am not very good at scary stories, so I don't write them."

Q: "What games did you like to play when you were a little boy?"

A: "My favourite game when I was little was hide-and-seek. I was very good at it because I could run very fast. There was a huge tree in my backyard that was always the home base."

Q: "Why did you start writing?"
Shaun

A: "I started writing so I would remember my stories."

Q: "What are some of your other hobbies, apart from storytelling?"

A: "Answering letters is a hobby for me. I also like to walk my dog off leash out in the woods. I like to ride my bicycle when the weather is nice. I like to climb trees — big white pine trees that go way up high above the rest of the forest."

Q: "There are a couple of songs on your CD. What kind of role do you think singing plays in communicating with kids, or the telling of a story?"

A: "I think of my stories as songs without music; they have the repetitive cadence of songs. Some of them even have music included, like in Mortimer, where he goes "CLANG, CLANG, RATTLE BING BANG!" The structure of singing works for kids before text does. So kids learn a lot about the structure of language

through what we call songs and
poetry. A baby's babbling is more like
a song. Songs and singing are integral
to the way kids learn language."

Q: "What are some ways to get kids
reading?"

A: "Make it fun; use funny voices and
sounds when you read to them. Make
it interesting for them; if they like
comic books, read comic books. It
doesn't have to be Shakespeare; any
kind of reading is good. If they want to
read books about motorcycles, then do
that with them. Books should expand a
child's current pastimes or hobbies,
whatever they're interested in."

Munsch Merits

**Some parents may express concern about the "tone"
of Munsch books. Emphasize that:**

- the humour comes from exaggeration, which has great appeal
for children.

- the stories take a zany approach to familiar childhood
experiences; they are fantasy, and children understand this.

- the humour often depends on situations where children get
the better of their parents or other authority figures. This kind
of role reversal is fun for children.

- children learn how the language and the illustrations combine
to capture the playfulness of the stories.

A Picture of Michael Martchenko

Michael Martchenko's art is well known to kids, parents and teachers across the country — and although he's illustrated books by lots of writers (including himself!), he is best known for his work with Robert Munsch.

Michael has always loved drawing. As a boy, he copied comic book covers, imitating the lines and colour. "It was great practice," he says. He was unable to take art classes in high school, but that didn't stop him. He still knew he wanted to be an artist, so he decided to study illustration at the Ontario College of Art in Toronto.

After graduating, Michael worked as a junior art director for an advertising company. His job was to work on storyboards, designing ads. That's where he thought he'd stay for the rest of his life. Then one day, at an art show, Robert saw Michael's work and was attracted to his lively style. He approached Michael to do the pictures for *The Paper Bag Princess*, and a terrific partnership was born.

At first, Michael didn't think much of the story. "My first reaction was 'Yuck!'" he says. He thought it was a typical fairy tale about a prince and princess. But then he read it and thought, "This is cool!"

But Michael didn't quit his advertising job at first. "I thought illustrating books was something I could do when I retired," he says. "I never thought about doing it full-time." So he would work during the day at the advertising agency, then spend the evenings and weekends working on his picture book illustrations.

Michael has now been creating picture books full-time for about ten years, and he couldn't be happier. "I love what I do," he says.

What's his secret to illustrating? When he first gets a story, Michael doesn't draw the sketches right away. Instead, he'll get what he calls "mind pictures" of what would work in the story. Then he'll do thumbnail sketches, or storyboards, just like he did when he was an art director. Full pencil drawings come next. Then the paintings are done in watercolours.

And what about the funny background images that his fans love? Well, he didn't always do them. As time went on, the ideas started to come to him. He didn't set out to have, say, a monkey helping other animals escape from the zoo, as in *Alligator Baby*. "They just happen," he says of the extra touches. Readers have come to expect them, but he believes that it's important to make sure that those background images aren't too distracting.

When he was doing the illustrations for *Mmm, Cookies!*, Michael started what has become a tradition in his books with Robert Munsch — he put in a pterodactyl. Robert liked it so much, he asked Michael to put it in all their books, and that's just what Michael does. (Look for it in four of the stories featured in this book.)

What does Michael like to do besides illustrate? He loves history and airplanes. In fact, he collects aviation material, like old uniforms and badges. He's created paintings of historical planes. He also recently picked up his guitar again. This helps him to relax a little from his busy schedule.

Michael Martchenko and Robert Munsch have developed a wonderful partnership, and their collaboration has brought great happiness to many people over the years. And, just as important, Michael has found great happiness himself.

"I still can't believe I'm doing this for a living," he says.

Adapted from *Munsch More!: A Robert Munsch Collection*

The story behind
Andrew's
Loose Tooth

The story of *Andrew's Loose Tooth* originated in Fort Qu'Appelle, Saskatchewan, in 1982. Robert Munsch told the story for a child who had four missing teeth. The story was a great success and he would often share it with young children who had loose teeth. But as time went on Robert Munsch didn't keep in touch with the original child who first inspired him to tell his story. Rather than letting this wonderful tale disappear he decided to substitute his own son, Andrew, as the main character in the book. He remembered that Andrew never liked his father trying to pull out his loose teeth. Would you?

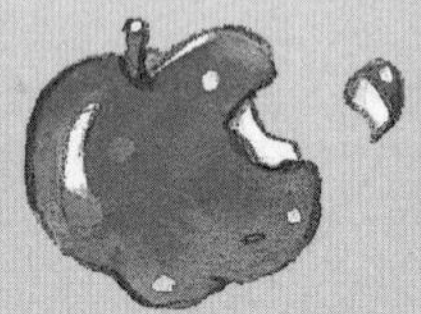

ANDREW'S LOOSE TOOTH

I liked the Part at the end When the tooth fairy got her tooth. Have you ever seen a tooth fairy on a motorbike?

by Traiden

Summary:

Andrew has a loose tooth and is determined that it will come out. Despite many attempts by his mother, father and dentist to pull out his tooth, it will not budge. So Andrew's friend Louis decides that it is time to call in a real expert: the tooth fairy. When she is unsuccessful, Louis finds the remedy. He gives Andrew some pepper to inhale, which brings on a great big sneeze that sends Andrew's tooth flying through the air.

Questions:

Before

Look at the front cover.
- Who do you think the two people on the front might be?
- Reading the title, can you think of a problem that might arise in this story?
- How do you think Andrew's tooth will eventually come out?
- Record the students' predictions on a chart.

Look at the back cover.
- What information can we find out about the author? the illustrator?

- Read the description on the back and predict who you think the real expert will be.
- Record the students' predictions on a chart.

During

- p. 6: Who do you think the dad might be?
- p. 14: What do you think the dentist is going to do?
- p. 18: What is Louis going to do?
- p. 22: What do you think Louis will suggest this time?

After

- Check the predictions you made before reading the book.
- On a chart, record the different ways that Andrew's mother, father and dentist tried to pull out his tooth.
- Look back at the illustration of the tooth fairy on page 21. Discuss with the students whether or not they think the tooth fairy in this story looks like tooth fairies in other stories that they have read.
- Looking at other books about tooth fairies (see List of Resources), use a Venn diagram to compare and contrast the tooth fairy in this story with the tooth fairies portrayed in other books.
- Why do you think the author made the tooth fairy in this book so different from tooth fairies in other stories?

Take a look

🌀 The boy in the story is Robert Munsch's son. Looking at the illustrations in this book, what can you learn about the author's family?

🌀 Point out the licence plate on the dentist's car on page 13.

How to Pull a Loose Tooth

In this activity the students will have the opportunity to use a sequence organizer to write about how they would attempt to pull a loose tooth.

Curriculum Link:
Language Arts — sequence writing

Materials:
Class set of Sequence Organizers (see reproducible on p. 12-13)

Procedure:
1. Begin by discussing with the children why our first teeth are called baby teeth. Ask the students about their experiences of losing a baby tooth: What were you doing when your tooth came out? Did it come out on its own or did you go to the dentist? Do you have a loose tooth right now? How many teeth have you lost? How did you lose a tooth?

2. Refer back to the chart describing the attempts that were made to pull Andrew's loose tooth. Remind the students that Robert Munsch stories are often funny because he tends to exaggerate situations that are too ridiculous to ever happen, e.g. the dentist ties one end of a rope to Andrew's tooth and the other end to his car.

3. With the children, brainstorm other solutions to Andrew's problem.

4. Explain to the students that they are going to write about how they would attempt to pull a tooth.

5. Begin by modelling orally a situation that requires a step-by-step procedure. For example, to make a snowman, first you . . . ; then you . . . ; after that . . . ; etc.

6. Select one of the attempts made in the story to pull Andrew's loose tooth, and fill out a sequence organizer together, e.g. how Andrew's father tries to pull out his tooth with a pair of pliers. Encourage the students to add details beyond those found in the illustrations and text.

7. Have the students select one of the ideas that you have brainstormed together and fill out their own sequence organizer using point form.

8. Using the sequence organizer that you filled out together, demonstrate for the students how to write up the information from the sequence organizer into a paragraph.

9. Have the students share their solutions with their classmates.

Literature Connections:

◎ Other books to share with the students might include:
  The Bear's Toothache by David McPhail
  Toot & Puddle: Charming Opal by Holly Hobbie
  The Tooth Fairy Tells All by Cynthia L. Copeland
  Tabitha's Terrifically Tough Tooth by Charlotte Middleton
  Wibble Wobble by Miriam Moss
  Doctor De Soto by William Steig

Sequence Organizer

Title: _______________________

Introduction (beginning sentence): _______________________

First

Then

After

Conclusion: _______________________

Name: ______________________________

____

____

Second
____
____
____

Next
____
____

Finally
____
____

Where Do Your Teeth Go?

Losing a tooth for the first time is a very exciting and sometimes traumatic experience for a young child. Many children follow the tradition of putting their teeth under their pillows in hopes that the tooth fairy will come. But what happens to their teeth? Where do they go? In this activity the students will have the opportunity to learn about the many different tooth traditions around the world and to write their own tradition.

Curriculum Link:
Language Arts — writing about experiences related to those in the story
                 — revising words and sentences

Materials:
Throw Your Tooth on the Roof: Tooth Traditions from Around the World by Selby B. Beeler
What Do the Fairies Do with All Those Teeth? by Michel Luppens and Philippe Beha
Class set of tooth-shaped organizers (see reproducible on p. 16)

Procedure:
1. Refer back to page 29 of *Andrew's Loose Tooth* and have the students suggest what they think the tooth fairy might do with Andrew's tooth.

2. Read aloud the story *What Do the Fairies Do with All Those Teeth?*.

3. Brainstorm with the children other ideas of what might happen to their teeth.

4. Ask each student to select one idea to write about. Then have each do a first draft for you to revise and edit. Once the writing has been edited, have each student do a good copy on tooth-shaped paper.

5. Have the students share their final copy with their classmates in the Author's Chair.

6. Create a display in your classroom to showcase the students' writing.

7. You may want to make a graph of how many teeth the students in your class have lost.

Extensions:

◎ Share the book *Throw Your Tooth on the Roof*. Identify some of the countries in the book and mark them on the map. Compare some of the similarities and differences of the tooth traditions in other countries to the Canadian tradition. You may have students in your class from other cultures who might like to share their traditions. Have the students create their own tooth tradition and write about it.

◎ Other books to share with the students might include:
Dear Tooth Fairy by Jane O'Connor
Dear Tooth Fairy by Alan Durant

After reading one or both of these books, have the students write a letter to the tooth fairy sharing their experiences of losing a tooth.

What Happened to
My Tooth

Name: _______________________________________

BOO!

Summary:

One Halloween Lance decides he wants to look so scary that people will scream and fall over when they see him. He paints his face and then covers it with a pillowcase. He goes trick-or-treating and when he reveals his face, people faint in fright. After going to only two houses, Lance has more treats than he can carry. A police officer who helps him take his bag home is so scared of Lance's face that he drives away. A teenager who comes to Lance's door screams and runs away, leaving his huge bag of candy behind. Lance ends up with enough candy to last him until . . . next Halloween.

Questions:

Before

Look at the front cover.
- At what time of the year do you think this story takes place?
- Who is the child scaring?
- Draw a quick sketch of the child's face.
- Why do you think the illustrator wouldn't show the child's face on the cover?

During

- Notice if your predictions were correct.
- p. 2: Why is Lance's father pleased that Lance wants to paint his face?
- p. 18: What is the police officer going to do?
- p. 22: Is the teenager going to scare Lance?

In June 1991 Robert Munsch made an unannounced visit to the Grade One/Two class at Lloyd George School in Hamilton, Ontario. Lance asked for a story about Halloween because it was his favourite day of the year. Robert Munsch made up the story that would later become *Boo!*. It changed as he told it to other children and wrote several versions. When he was ready to publish the story, the school had closed and Lance had moved back to Jamaica. Robert Munsch could not talk to Lance or take photographs, as he usually does. But one interesting detail about Lance's neighbourhood was included in the illustrations for *Boo!*: the school was located beside a steel mill, and the mill appears in several pictures in the book.

- Was Lance's face scary? Why?
- Why do you think Lance wanted to look so scary?
- Why didn't the police officer say anything to Lance about stealing the candy and food?
- Lance does some things that aren't really funny in real life. What makes the story funny, then? Would the story be as funny if it had "realistic" illustrations or photographs instead of Michael Martchenko's cartoon-like illustrations?

Take a look

Make sure you give children the chance to examine and enjoy the illustrations. In this story children should notice . . .

- the father fixing a costume with tools from his toolkit on page 3.

- quirky details, such as the furnished birdcage and playful mice on page 11, the pterodactyl in the mailbox on page 19, etc.

- the large industrial plant behind the houses in Lance's neighbourhood.

Scary Masks

This activity gives students an opportunity to experiment with colour, texture and a variety of materials to create their own scary masks.

Curriculum Link:
Art — using colour, pattern and texture for a visual effect

Materials:
Paper plates for face outlines

Coloured felt pens or crayons

Construction paper

Fabrics with interesting textures

Wool

Pipe cleaners

Ribbon

Glue

Scissors

Procedure:
1. Review the descriptions of Lance's scary face on pages 4 and 6 and the illustration on pages 26 and 27. Discuss what makes Lance's face scary.

2. Let children create scary faces out of the paper plates. They can use any materials to draw and create their faces. Materials such as fabric can be glued on. Features can "pop out" of the face using pipe cleaners or folded paper.

Extensions:
◎ Students can design their own masks out of papier mâché.

◎ Students can create their own scary whole-body portraits. Have them trace their bodies on large pieces of butcher paper and use the materials to create a costume as well as a scary face.

Halloween Safety

Lance and the other children pictured in *Boo!* demonstrate some safe and some unsafe Halloween practices. In this activity, children will create posters to remind others of safe ways to enjoy Halloween.

Curriculum Link:

Health — safety
Art

Materials:

Poster paper
Paints or coloured felt pens
Halloween-themed cut-outs, e.g. pumpkins, bats

Procedure:

1. Remind students that *Boo!* takes place at Halloween. Quickly scan the story and illustrations again and ask students to identify the things that Lance does that are safe (e.g. paints his face rather than wear a mask), and the things that are unsafe (e.g. puts a pillowcase over his head). Record their observations on a T-chart on the board.

2. Brainstorm other safe and unsafe Halloween practices. Some good examples of safe practices include:

◉ Put makeup on your face instead of wearing a mask

◉ Trick-or-treat in a group and with an adult or older teenager to supervise

◉ Trick-or-treat along a familiar route

◉ Carry a flashlight

◉ Don't cut across yards or alleys

◉ Stay on the sidewalks

◉ Walk; don't run

◉ Cross streets safely

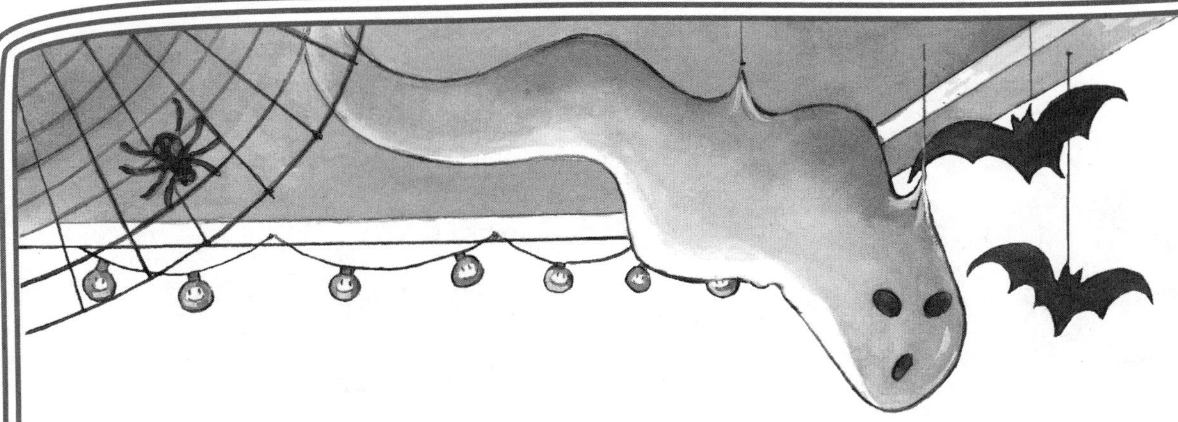

- Make sure your costume is fireproof

- Make sure your costume is visible at night (bright colours, reflective strip)

- Make sure you can move and see properly in your costume

- Don't carry any dangerous props

- Only go to houses with porch lights on

- Don't enter any house; stay on the porch to accept your treats

- Don't use candles in jack-o'-lanterns

- Don't eat any treats until you come home and an adult has checked them

3. Brainstorm safety tips for adults to remember at Halloween, such as driving slowly in residential areas and lighting up front porches.

4. Allow each child to create a poster advertising one Halloween safety tip. Place the posters in hallways and around the school in the weeks before Halloween to remind students to stay safe.

Extensions:

- Students could record public service announcements or brief commercials that advertise their Halloween safety tips. The tips could be broadcast over the school PA system in the days before Halloween.

- UNICEF Canada promotes safe Halloween practices through their Partners for Safety programme. They work with local police, fire, ambulance and media across Canada. Inquire about their materials for use in schools.

MMM, COOKIES!

Mmm Cookies

I liked it when Christopher came into the school and took a bite of the play clay cookie. His face turned three different colors green, red and blue.

— By Jakelynne

Summary:

Christopher finds a huge pile of play clay in the basement and decides to make some cookies. He shares the cookies with his parents, who quickly discover that they aren't real. They run to the bathroom to wash the taste out of their mouths. As soon as Christopher leaves for school they quickly call his teacher to warn her that he may be giving out play clay cookies. She tells them not to worry and assures them that she knows just what to do. She makes Christopher his own play clay cookie to try. After he from washes out his mouth, the class makes a batch of real cookies and Christopher takes his real cookie home to his parents.

Questions:

Before

Look at the front cover.
- Do you think that the cookies are real? Why or why not?
- Why do you think Christopher's parents are looking so disgusted?

- What do you think Christopher's parents are thinking?
- How do you think these cookies would taste?
- Would you describe these cookies as "mmm, good"?

Look at the dedication page.
- Why do you think the image of the two mice
  was chosen to illustrate the dedication page?
- Do you think that it is a clue as to what the
  story is about?
- Do you think the mice will be in the story?

Look at the back cover.
- Share the information on the back cover about the author and illustrator.
- Read the description on the back of the book.
- Who do you think Christopher will choose to try out his play clay cookie?
- What would you do if someone offered you a play clay cookie?

During

- p. 18: What do you think the teacher will do?
- p. 26: Where do you think Christopher will take his cookie?

After

- Ask the students to recall their experiences with making pretend cookies out of playdough or Plasticine.
- Make a batch of "Mom's Play Clay" using the recipe at the beginning of the book.
- Depending on the time of year, the students could make a playdough gift for a special occasion, e.g. a Christmas ornament, a charm for Mother's Day or a pencil holder for Father's Day.
- The playdough could also be applied to another area of the curriculum, e.g. creating an inuksuk for an Inuit study.

Take a look

Can you find other Robert Munsch books or characters from his other stories in the illustrations?

Acts of Kindness

Helping students to develop the virtue of kindness will help them to become more compassionate and to think of others. In this activity students will have the opportunity to offer their help to others and to recognize when others are displaying kindness toward them.

Curriculum Link:

Health — relationship choices

Materials:

Acts of Kindness slips of paper (see reproducible on p. 26)
Box for the slips, labelled "Acts of Kindness"

Procedure:

1. Begin by asking the students if they think that sometimes we can be unkind and yet we don't intentionally mean to hurt anyone. We just think we are being funny. Could playing a joke on someone ever be considered an unkind act?

2. Ask the students to recall something in the story that Christopher did that would be considered an unkind act.

3. Invite the children to share a time when someone did something to them that was unkind. Ask: How did that make you feel? What did you do?

4. Refer back to the story and ask the children if they felt one of the characters in the story had displayed an act of kindness. Have the children describe a time that someone was kind to them. Ask: What did they do for you? How did that make you feel?

5. Explain to the students that they are going to have the opportunity to display an act of kindness to a family member or friend.

6. Brainstorm with the children something kind that they could do for another person, e.g. open the door or help set the table for dinner. Record these on chart paper.

7. Have the students select one idea from the chart and fill out an Act of Kindness slip. Tell the students not to put their name on the slip.

8. Place the slips of paper in a mystery box labelled "Acts of Kindness" and have each student draw out a slip. If they pull out their own paper have them return it to the box and draw again.

9. Explain to the children that they have 24 hours to carry out their Act of Kindness.

10. After the 24 hours is over, have the students share with the class the kind act that they did for a family member, friend or neighbour.

Extension:

◎ As a follow-up to this activity you could have a "Peer Catching Peers" week where the children catch their peers displaying an act of kindness. If they observe their peers carrying out a kind act, e.g. helping someone at recess or inviting someone to play, they could fill out an Act of Kindness slip (see reproducible). At the end of the week you could share some of the kind acts the students caught their peers performing and have a draw for a prize.

Literature Connections:

◎ Other books to share with the students might include:
How Kind, by Mary Murphy
Glenna's Seeds, by Nancy Edwards
I Like Your Buttons!, by Sarah Marwil Lamstein

Acts of Kindness

How Many Cookies in the Cookie Jar?

In this activity the students will be learning a math game as an introduction to the concept of multiplication. This game could be played with the whole class or it could be placed at a math centre for students to play with a partner.

Curriculum Link:
Math — introduction to multiplication

Materials:
Dice
Class set of booklets of blank paper

Preparation:
Make up booklets ahead of time — 8 blank sheets stapled together

Procedure:
1. Explain to the students that they are going to learn a new game that they will play with a partner as an introduction to multiplication.

2. Invite one of the students to help you demonstrate how to play the game.

3. Begin by rolling the die — the number you roll represents the number of cookie jars you draw on the first page of your booklet. Your partner then rolls the die and on her first page draws pictures of that many cookie jars. The first person rolls a second time and the number this time is the number of cookies to draw inside each jar. The second person then takes a turn. Once you both have cookies in your jars, you count the number of cookies you each have and the person with the highest number wins that round.

4. Continue taking turns rolling the die to complete all 8 pages.

5. When the students have completed their booklets, the teacher will demonstrate how to write the multiplication sentence to go with each picture, e.g. if you had 4 jars with 2 cookies in each jar, you would write 4 x 2 = 8.

Extensions:

◉ Make a batch of real cookies with the children. You could begin by reading *A Cow, a Bee, a Cookie, and Me* by Meredith Hooper. This story explains where in nature the different ingredients needed to make the cookies come from. A recipe for Honey Cookies is included in the book.

◉ Have each student bring a favourite cookie recipe from home to share with the class. Ask the students to illustrate their cookie recipes. Compile the recipes and pictures, and photocopy them to create special books for each student to take home.

SMELLY SOCKS

Summary:

Tina wants a new pair of socks. When her mother takes her to the only store in town, they discover that all they have are black socks. Tina's grandfather rows her across the river to buy the perfect pair of red, yellow and green socks. Tina loves her new socks so much that she refuses to take them off. But after a few days the socks begin to smell and her friends decide to take her down to the river and wash them. Tina is so pleased with her clean socks that she asks her mom for a shirt to match. If she wears it long enough, maybe her friends will wash it, too!

Questions:

Before

Look at the front cover.
  • Where do you think this story takes place? Does the picture give you a clue?

Look at the back cover.
  • Read the description on the back and predict what action you think Tina's friends will have to take.
  • Record the students' predictions on a chart.
  • Read the information about the author.
  • Who did Robert Munsch have in mind when he created this story?
  • Mark the Hay River Dene Reserve (Katl'odeeche), Northwest Territories, on a map.

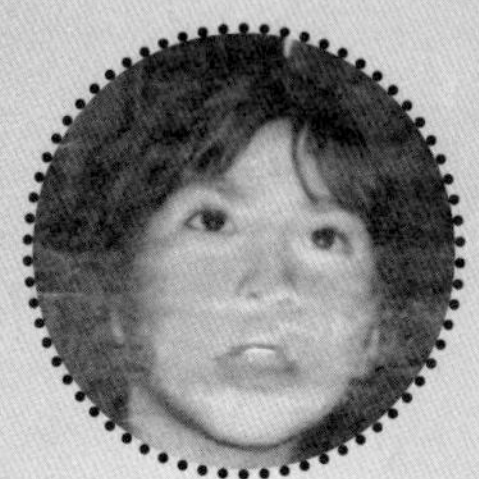

The story behind Smelly Socks

While on tour of the Canadian High Arctic in 1984, Robert Munsch visited the Hay River Dene Reserve. A little girl named Tina was one of three children who came to hear his stories. She was wearing very colourful socks. That day Robert Munsch made up a story about Tina called "Dirty Socks." In the story Tina exchanged dirty socks for other people's clean socks. Over the years he continued to tell the sock story and over the years it changed. Eventually his editor suggested that he publish it. Robert Munsch contacted a friend in Hay River who sent him photographs of Tina at age six and photographs of the reserve. He gave these to Michael Martchenko, who used the pictures to help him create his illustrations of the buildings and backgrounds in the book. When the book was ready, Robert Munsch was invited back to the reserve to launch the book in the place where the story began in 1984.

Look at the dedication page.
  - How does the picture of the beavers give us a clue as to what the story
    might be about?

  - p. 6: Why is Tina having trouble steering the boat?
  - p. 13: Why does the grandfather look sick?
  - p. 14: What do you think will happen if Tina never takes off her socks?
  - p. 24: Do you think that Tina will continue to wear clean socks?
  - p. 25: Why do you think the illustrator chose to draw flowers
    surrounding the clean socks?

  - Check the predictions you made before reading
    the book.
  - Refer back to Hay River on the map. What lake is it
    on? Is there a city across the lake?

Take a look

Before you begin reading the story, explain to the students
that the pterodactyl is a symbol that Michael Martchenko
continues to include in Munsch books. While reading the
story have the students look for the pterodactyl.

Many of the illustrations in the story feature modern
buildings or items as well as traditional ones. Take the class
on a scavenger hunt through the illustrations and record on
a T-chart the modern and traditional items that you find.

Research Project on Northern Animals

In this activity students will have the opportunity to research many of the northern animals found in the book. Depending on your students' experience with research projects this may be done as a whole class experience, recording key facts and ideas together, or students may work in small groups to research animals found in the north.

Curriculum Link:

Language Arts — developing research skills
Science — animal life cycles
Social Studies — northern community

Materials:

Class set of Research Webs (see reproducible on p. 34-35)
Information books on northern animals

Websites:

http://collections.ic.gc.ca/arctic/species/species.htm
http://www.enchantedlearning.com/coloring/arcticanimals.shtml

Procedure:

1. Refer back to the picture of the northern animals on page 27 of the book. With the students, brainstorm a list of animals that appear in the story and record these on a chart. You may want to add to your list some additional northern animals not found in the story, e.g. polar bear, caribou, white-tailed deer.

2. Explain to the students that they are going to have the opportunity to learn more about northern animals.

3. Select one of the animals to explore with the class as a research project. Brainstorm questions that they may have about the animal you have selected and record these questions on a chart. Looking at the questions, divide them into categories, e.g. description, enemies, food, habitat, protection and interesting facts.

4. Focus on one category at a time. With the children, share the information books on the category you have selected for that particular day. Record the facts on chart paper.

5. Model for the students how to take the information on that category from the chart and transfer it in point form to a research web. You may want to make an overhead of the web to use for the demonstration.

6. Once the web is completed, demonstrate for the students how to write up the information from each category into a paragraph.

a) One format:
The students could write each paragraph on a separate sheet of paper so that it could be stapled together in the form of a booklet with each paragraph as a chapter. Each of the categories could be illustrated. To complete their report the students could add a table of contents, a title page and an "about the author" page.

b) Another format:
Each child could use a large piece of bristol board to display their information, illustrating each category.

Extension:

◎ Students could select another northern animal to research with a partner or in a small group. The students could present their projects to the rest of the class and compare and contrast some of the similarities and differences among the animals.

Reference Books for Research Project:

All About Canadian Animals Series (14 vols.) by Barb McDermott
The Bear Family by Bev Harvey
Beavers by Leonard Lee Rue
Canada's Arctic Animals by Chelsea Donaldson
Wildlife Series *(Beavers; Deer, Moose, Elk and Caribou; Bears: Polar Bears, Black Bears and Grizzly Bears)* by Deborah Hodge

Research Web

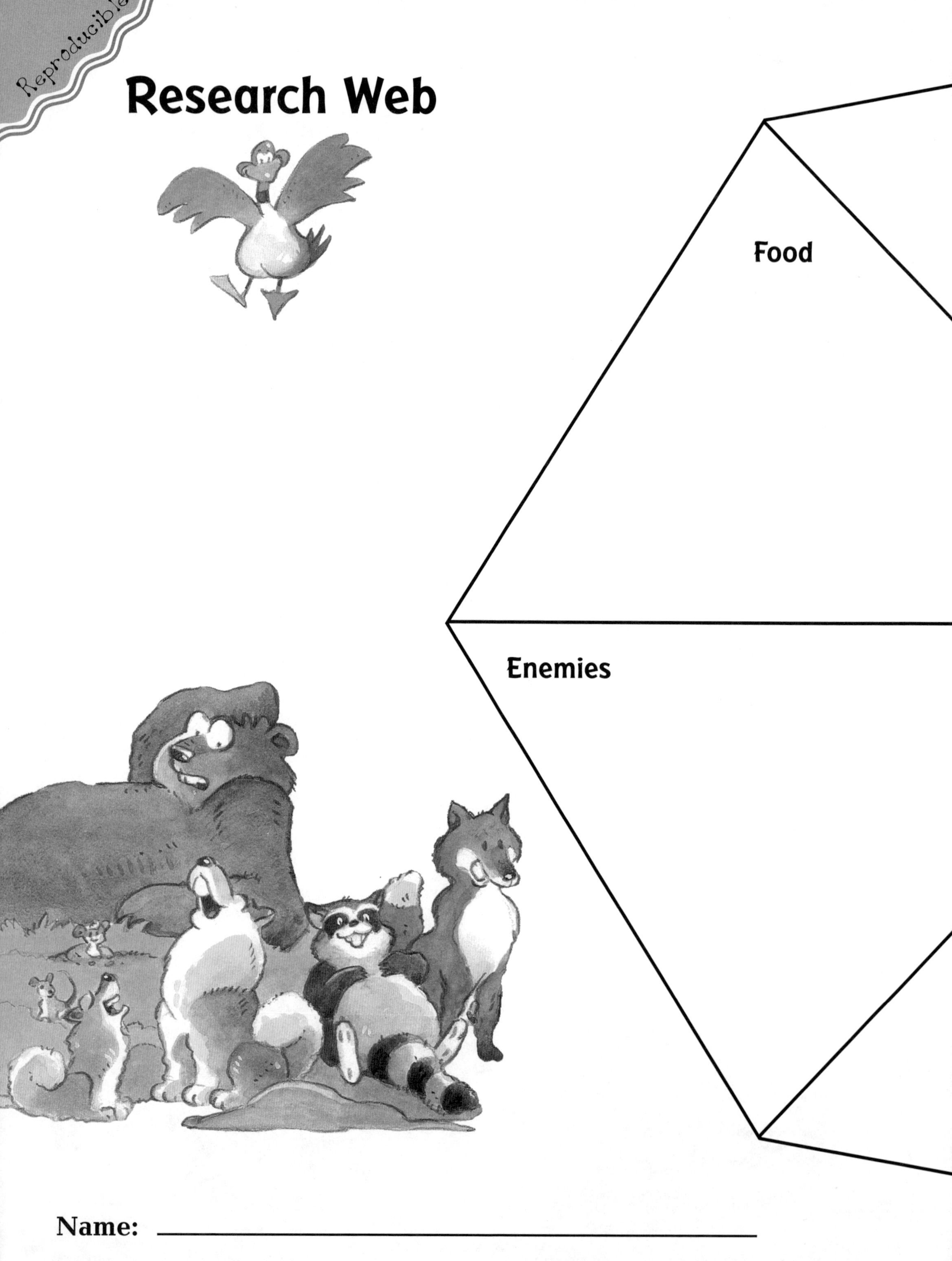

Name: _______________________________

Description

Protection

Interesting
Facts

Habitat

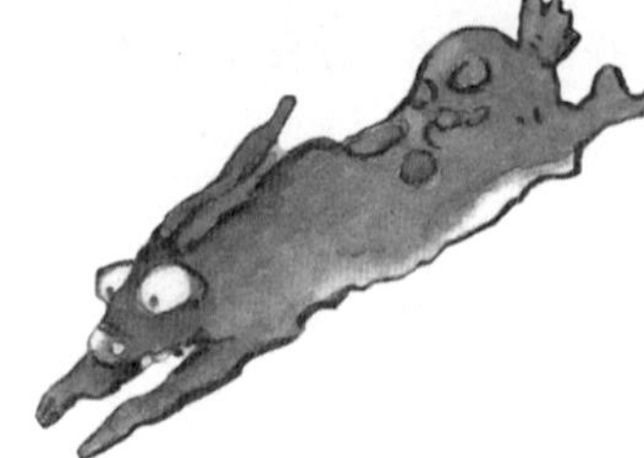

Buoyancy and Boats

In this activity, students will design a boat that will float, and perform a test to see how much weight their boat can hold before it sinks.

Curriculum Link:

Science — buoyancy and boats, constructing a boat that will float, evaluating and testing various designs

Math — estimating, measuring and recording mass (weight) using non-standard units

Materials:

Plasticine (a small ball for each student)
6 large containers of water
6 varieties of weights, e.g. pennies, small plastic cubes, etc.
6 collection boxes
Slips of paper
Pencils

Preparation:

Set up 6 stations around the room, each with a large container of water, a collection box (for predictions), slips of paper (to record predictions), pencils and a set of weights.

Procedure:

1. Remind the students that in the story *Smelly Socks*, Tina and her grandfather rowed across the lake to buy Tina's socks. Explain to the children that each of them is going to have the opportunity to design and make their own boat. Their task will be to see how much weight their boat can hold before it sinks.

2. Demonstrate for the students how to build a boat by shaping a small ball of Plasticine.

3. Point out to the students the stations that are set up around the room. Tell the students that once they have finished designing their boats, they will be going to each station in turn to predict the number of weights they think their boats will hold.

4. Have them record their name and their prediction at each station on a slip of paper.

5. After the children have recorded their predictions, have each test their boat at each station and record the number of weights it can actually hold before sinking. Have the students deposit their slips in the box.

6. As a whole class, discuss the results of the experiment. How close were your predictions? Did the number of weights your boat would hold vary at each station? Why? Which shape floated the best? Did the shape of the boat determine how much weight it would hold?

7. Ask two students with different-shaped boats to share their results with the class. Did their boats hold the same amount of weight? Why or why not? Compare other boat designs made by the students.

Extension:

◎ Ask the students if they have ever experienced riding in a boat or canoe. Looking at page 7 and 8 of the story, ask the students to identify any safe or unsafe boating practices. Brainstorm other boating safety tips with the students, e.g. plan your trip, including the time you will return; always travel with an adult; and operate at a safe speed.

This book started as a simple phrase that Robert Munsch used to say to very young children. He would raise his hands up, up and then faaaaall down on the ground. The children thought it was hilarious and played along. The phrase, and the actions that went with it, were incorporated into this story about climbing. Note how the phrase "up, up, down" is printed on the page so that readers will use their voices correctly! Anna, the child featured in the story, was a neighbour of Robert Munsch's.

UP, UP, DOWN

Summary:

Anna loves to climb. She climbs refrigerators, dressers, and trees. Her parents tell her, "Be careful! Don't climb!" — because she also falls down. But Anna doesn't listen. One day, in an effort to get her down from a tree, her mom and dad both try to climb the tree. And they both fall down. Now Anna is saying, "Be careful! Don't climb!"

Questions:

Before

Look at the front cover.
- What is this girl doing?
- Why do you think the story is called *Up, Up, Down?*

Look at the back cover and read the description.
- Predict how you think Anna's parents are going to get her down.

Look at the dedication page.
- Who is the girl on the dedication page?

During

- p. 6: What does Anna find to climb?
- p. 12: What is Anna going to do at the top of the tree?
- p. 20: How are Anna's parents going to get her out of the tree?

• Why does Anna like to climb?

Take a look

Make sure you give children the chance to examine and enjoy the illustrations. This book includes covers of other Munsch/Martchenko books, pictures on the walls of other tall things Anna would like to climb, and funny animals in the tree. Notice, too, some of the interesting ways the illustrations enhance the effect of the story, e.g. the two-page vertical spread of the tall tree, and the stars around the characters showing the impact of the fall.

Climbing Trees, Reaching Goals

This activity is intended to span several weeks or even months as students work toward their goals.

Curriculum Link:
Health — goal-setting

Materials:
Class set of leaf-shaped organizers to record short- and long-term goals (see reproducible on p. 42)

Procedure:
1. Ask the children why they think Anna likes to climb. Ask them if they have ever felt really proud after accomplishing some goal, e.g. riding a two-wheel bike, sliding down the firefighter's pole at the playground, or learning something difficult at school.

2. Explain that often we talk about things we would like to accomplish — our goals — as mountains to climb.

3. Explain that we are going to create our own special classroom tree that will help us celebrate the goals we have set for ourselves and accomplished.

4. List some examples of your own goals to illustrate the concept.

5. Explain that you can only meet your goals if you have a plan to get there. For example:

My goal is to spell all my spelling words correctly on our weekly spelling quiz.
My plan is to practise spelling the words every night after supper this week.

6. Distribute a reproducible leaf outline to each student. Ask them to write a goal on the leaf. They also need to identify some way to meet that goal. They can decorate or colour their leaf if they wish.

7. As students reach their goals, display their leaves on a tree on the bulletin board. Don't forget a round of applause and a cheer for every goal that has been met!

Extension:

◉ You might discuss the difference between short-term goals — things we can accomplish quite quickly — and long-term goals — things that we have to work on for a longer time before we can accomplish them. List some examples of your own short- and long-term goals to illustrate the difference. You might also have students identify the personal quality they have that will help them reach their goals, like strength, perseverance, courage, even stubbornness!

Literature Connections:

Stories of children demonstrating important qualities of character and meeting their goals include:

Amazing Grace by Mary Hoffman

Chin Chiang and the Dragon's Dance by Ian Wallace

JoJo's Flying Side Kick by J. Brian Pinkney

Mirette on the High Wire by Emily Arnold McCully

My Goal

Teaching with Robert Munsch Books, Vol. 2, p. 42 © 2005 Scholastic Canada Ltd.

Name: _______________________________

We Love Trees

Curriculum Link:
Science — seasonal change, conservation

Materials:
Paper and crayons for tree bark rubbings
A small journal or notebook
Coloured pencils or crayons for drawings
Measuring tape

Procedure:
1. Identify a tree in the schoolyard or a nearby forested area that students can adopt and observe over the school year.

2. When a tree is selected, allow students to make a rubbing of the tree bark. This rubbing can become the cover of their "Tree Book" in which they can record their observations of the tree.

3. For the first observation, ask children to write a description of the tree and guess what kind of tree it is. They could also draw a picture of the tree and guess what kinds of animals they think might rely on it for food, shelter etc. Watch the tree carefully. Do you see spiders? Squirrels? Birds? Touch the tree. What does it feel like? Does it have leaves or needles? What does the tree smell like? Have students record their observations. They could also measure the circumference of the tree trunk and even estimate its height.

4. Give children the opportunity to observe the tree once a month over the school year, each time sketching the tree, making observations of the tree and writing how it has changed.

5. Students could also do research about that kind of tree, other places it grows, its uses and other facts about the tree. They could conduct research about the animals that live in or use the tree.

6. At the end of the year, their notes can be compiled into a completed "Tree Book."

Extensions:

◉ Students could plant their own trees.

◉ Art connections include creating objects with leaf shapes or drawing trees with pastels.

Literature Connections:

There are many good stories about trees, including:
A Forest of Stories: Magical Tree Tales from Around the World
  by Rina Singh
The Giving Tree by Shel Silverstein
Leo's Tree by Debora Pearson
Once There Was a Tree by Natalia Romanova
A Tree for Me by Nancy Van Laan

Some non-fiction titles that help children learn more about trees include:
Are Trees Alive? by Debbie S. Miller
Be a Friend to Trees by Patricia Lauber
Have You Seen Trees? by Joanne Oppenheim
Learn About Trees by Peter Mellett
Tell Me, Tree: All About Trees for Kids by Gail Gibbons
A Tree Is Growing by Arthur Dorros

A wonderful book that illustrates a tree's changes through the seasons is:
Sky Tree: Seeing Science Through Art by Thomas Locker

ZOOM!

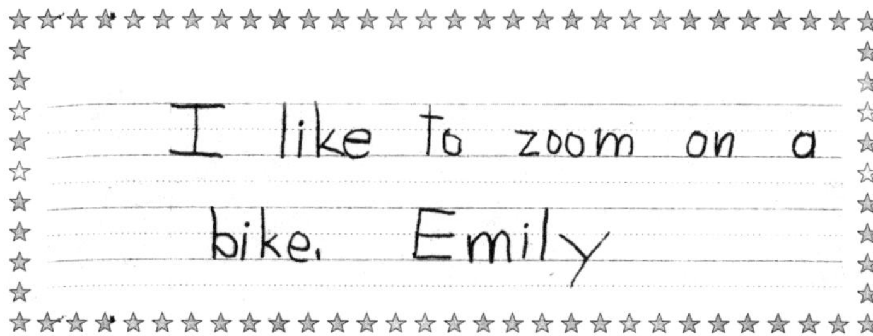

Summary:

Lauretta's old wheelchair needs to be replaced, so her mother takes her to buy a new one. The wheelchair store has a nice five-speed, a ten-speed and a fifteen-speed wheelchair, but Lauretta wants the 92-speed, black, silver and red, dirt-bike wheelchair. Her mother agrees to let her try it out, but she gets a speeding ticket on her first test drive. Her parents are upset about the speeding ticket, but when Lauretta's brother has an emergency and has to get to the hospital quickly, Lauretta proves how handy her speedy wheelchair can be.

Questions:

Before

Look at the front cover.
- Why do you think the story is called *Zoom!*?
- Why are the police chasing the girl in the wheelchair?

Look at the back cover and read the description.
- Predict what you think is going to happen when Lauretta goes really, really fast.

Look at the dedication page.
- What do you notice about Lauretta?

During

(Note: In order for students to predict some of the major events in the story, read each page before showing children the accompanying illustration.)
- p. 10: What kind of wheelchair does Lauretta want?
- p. 14: What is going to happen when Lauretta takes the wheelchair on the road?

Zoom! is a story that has been about many different things: bicycles, skateboards, wheelchairs, just about anything that children like to ride. The first time Robert Munsch told this story, it was about a boy from Calgary who got a speeding ticket riding his bicycle. He changed the story every time he told it to a different audience, but he always made it be about a wheelchair if there was a child in a wheelchair listening to him. In 1997, Lauretta from Orillia, Ontario, wrote to Robert Munsch and asked him to write a story about a girl who walks with crutches and uses a wheelchair, as she does. He was glad to turn *Zoom!* into a special story for Lauretta.

- p. 18: What are her parents going to say about the ticket?
- p. 24: Why won't the car start? How is Lauretta's brother going to get to the hospital?
- p. 28: Why doesn't Lauretta want that wheelchair anymore?

- Draw a picture of the wheelchair Lauretta wants, and then look at the illustration on page 30.
- Why do you think Lauretta wants to go really, really fast?
- Robert Munsch says that this story wasn't originally about a girl's wheelchair. It was about a boy and his bicycle. If this story was about you, what kind of transportation would it be about?

Take a look

🌀 Make sure you give children the chance to examine and enjoy the illustrations. This book includes the usual Martchenko zany trademarks: small animals doing funny things, Santa peeking out of a doorway, the pterodactyl, the robber in the police car reading another Munsch book.

Convince Me!

This activity gives students an opportunity to construct a well-reasoned, persuasive argument.

Curriculum Link:
Language Arts — persuasive writing

Materials:
Convince Me organizer (see reproducible on p. 49)

Procedure:
1. Draw a T-chart on the board. On one side, print BUY the 92-speed wheelchair; on the other side, print DON'T BUY the 92-speed wheelchair.

2. Review *Zoom!*. Draw children's attention to page 12, where Lauretta's mother lists three reasons why she should not have the fast wheelchair: it costs too much money; it goes too fast; Lauretta is too little for such a wheelchair. Write those reasons in the DON'T BUY column of the T-chart.

3. Have the children brainstorm reasons to buy the wheelchair, as well as any other reasons for not buying it. List their suggestions in the chart.

4. Encourage partners or small groups to discuss different points of view by having them share their opinions about whether or not Lauretta's mother should buy the wheelchair.

5. Ask each group to agree on an opinion and complete the reproducible to organize their arguments. (You could use Lauretta's mother's opinion and the three reasons she gives as an example to demonstrate how to use the organizer.)

6. Ask the children to pretend they are Lauretta. Ask them to write a letter to her parents explaining why they should (or should not) buy the wheelchair. Have them use the organizer to help them in their writing.

Extensions:

- Groups having opposite opinions could try to persuade each other.

- Children could use the reproducible to organize another persuasive argument for their principal or their parents.

Literature Connections:

For an excellent non-fiction example of children's persuasive writing, see:
Should We Have Pets? A Persuasive Text by Sylvia Lollis et al.

Name: ____

Convince Me

We think that ___________________________________

____

____

Reason 1: ___________________________________

____

Reason 2: ___________________________________

____

Reason 3: ___________________________________

____

Our final decision is that _______________________

____

____

Building Empathy

Empathy is identifying with and understanding others' feelings. Educator and author Michele Borba calls it "the first essential virtue of moral intelligence." *Zoom!* is a good discussion starter about empathy, because it features a character who faces physical challenges, but also has obvious gifts. It will help children appreciate that having empathy for someone does not mean pitying them.

Curriculum Link:
Health — personal relationships
Character education

Materials:
T-chart organizer (see reproducible on p. 53)

Procedure:
1. Ask children if they have ever cried watching a movie or TV show when something sad happened to a character, or cheered when something really nice happened. Discuss why they were able to feel what those characters were feeling.

2. Explain that empathy means being able to understand and appreciate how someone else is feeling.

3. Ask children to think about real-life examples of times they understood how someone else was feeling, perhaps when a friend was hurt by someone's mean words. Discuss what kinds of things they do when they feel empathy for someone. For example, if they see a child excluded from a game on the playground, they might offer to play a different game with them in order to make them feel better.

4. Talk about Lauretta's disability. Try to imagine what it is like for her. What would be the hardest part about being in a wheelchair? How do you suppose people would treat her sometimes? Why do you think she would like to go fast?

5. In order to help children understand that having empathy does not mean feeling sorry for Lauretta, brainstorm with students the things they know about Lauretta after reading the story. They may include information such as: she is not able to walk; she is brave; she is quick-thinking. Help them appreciate that while Lauretta may face challenges, she also has many gifts.

6. To continue to build children's empathy, over the next several weeks work with the children to increase their awareness and use of the vocabulary of feelings, an important first step in building empathy. Children could create a "Feelings Alphabet" book or a word wall, where they identify and illustrate a "feelings" word for every letter of the alphabet, e.g. A is for afraid, B is for bored, and so on.

7. Give students the opportunity to enhance their sensitivity to others by reading other stories about characters who face special challenges and discussing what it would be like to be those characters. Some suggestions are listed under Literature Connections.

8. Finally, provide opportunities for students to consider other people's points of view. They could complete a "Thought in the Head" organizer about a character in a story. They could do a role-playing exercise, e.g. two children having a minor disagreement could be asked to exchange shoes and then articulate the other person's point of view, literally "walking in someone else's shoes."

9. Once students have had some experience thinking about empathy, complete a T-chart with the children in which they list what empathy looks like, and what it sounds like. Some suggestions might include:

<table>
<tr><th>Empathy looks like . . .</th><th>Empathy sounds like . . .</th></tr>
<tr><td>*Hugging someone who is crying*</td><td>*"Good job! I know you tried really hard."*</td></tr>
<tr><td>*Comforting someone who is sick*</td><td>*"Can I help you?"*</td></tr>
<tr><td>*Inviting someone to play with you*</td><td>*"Are you OK?"*</td></tr>
<tr><td>*Cheering when someone else wins*</td><td>*"I'm really excited for you."*</td></tr>
</table>

Extension:

◎ Students could use the ideas in the T-chart to create "Empathy is" posters to display in school hallways.

Literature Connections:

There are many good picture books that lend themselves to a discussion about how people with disabilities feel, such as:

Arnie and the New Kid by Nancy Carlson
Hooway for Wodney Wat! by Helen Lester
Rolling Along: the Story of Taylor and His Wheelchair
  by Jamee Riggio Heelan
Sammy Wakes His Dad by Chip Emmons
Way to Go, Alex! by Robin Pulver

Some non-fiction titles that help children understand the realities facing children with physical challenges include:

Being in a Wheelchair by Lois Keith
Some Kids Use Wheelchairs by Lola M. Schaefer

For more information about enhancing children's moral intelligence, see:

Building Moral Intelligence by Michele Borba, which is the source for some of the lesson ideas listed here.

Name: _______________________________

Empathy looks like . . .	Empathy sounds like . . .

We Like the Sound of Munsch!

After reading and listening to many Munsch books, help your students incorporate sound effects into their own writing with this activity.

Curriculum Link:

Language Arts

Materials:

CD *Love You Forever: The Best of Robert Munsch* (2003)
"Tell Me a Story" Munsch book-and-CD or book-and-cassette packages
http://www.robertmunsch.com
Sounds Like Munsch strips (see reproducible on p. 57)
Copies of Robert Munsch books (with relevant page numbers marked)

Procedure:

1. Distribute the strips to several students.

2. Ask them to read the excerpt typed on the strip they have been given. (These are short selections from Munsch titles, typed in regular type rather than the modified type in the actual books. If they have not heard the books before, they will probably read the text in a relatively unexpressive way.)

3. Listen to the same stories (or excerpts from the stories) on Robert Munsch's website, cassette, or CD. Ask students to observe how Munsch's telling of the stories is different from the readings done by the students. Students should notice that Robert Munsch is extremely expressive when he tells his stories. He uses his voice in funny ways and adds a lot of sound effects. This is in fact where much of the humour of his stories comes from. Often the stories he tells are also slightly different from those we might know in the books. Discuss these differences with the students.

4. Robert Munsch stories in books beg to be read aloud to children. Ask the students how someone might write the stories in a way that would encourage the readers to use their voices in a dramatic or funny or expressive way when reading them to children. Look at the marked pages of the Munsch books and see how the typeface, size, arrangement and punctuation would encourage readers to read the stories in a particularly expressive way or make certain sound effects. For example: the phrase "up, up, down" in the book is actually printed with the letters rising up and falling down, to encourage readers to do the same with their voices; the word "zoom" is extended in print to encourage readers to make longer and louder "zoom"s as they read. Practise reading these excerpts with the appropriate sound effects.

5. Explore other Munsch titles and make a list of all the sound effects you can find in his books.

6. Explore books other than those by Robert Munsch that use sound effects, and discuss how and why the authors use them, and how they are printed in a way that would help you know how to read them. (Some book suggestions are listed in Literature Connections.)

7. Play some tape recordings of sounds students might recognize from home, the classroom, the school or the community. Ask them to guess what each sound is, and then try to create ways of writing out each sound. What does it sound like when someone jumps into the pool? How would you write down the sound of milk being poured into a cereal bowl? What word would best capture the sound of someone writing with chalk on a blackboard?

8. Give students the opportunity to incorporate sound effects into their own writing, in poems or stories.

Extensions:

◎ Once a lengthy list has been created, ask children to identify their favourite Munsch sound effect and explain why they like it.

◎ Older students could be introduced to the concept of onomatopoeia and look for examples in the Munsch books. They could be challenged to distinguish between examples of onomatopoeia and the use of sound effects.

◎ Have a fun contest to see who can tell a Munsch story most expressively.

◎ Turn a Munsch story into a Readers' Theatre presentation. Assign parts and have the students present it at a school assembly.

Literature Connections:

Achoo! Bang! Crash! A Noisy Alphabet by Ross McDonald
Busy, Busy City Street by Cari Meister
Crash! Bang! Boom! A Book of Sounds by Peter Spier
It's My City: A Singing Map by April Pulley Sayre
Slop Goes the Soup: A Noisy Warthog Word Book
    by Pamela Duncan Edwards
We're Going on a Bear Hunt by Michael Rosen
The Wheels on the Bus by Paul O. Zelinsky

Sounds like Munsch

Anna went up, up, up, up, up, up . . . fall down. And landed right on her bottom. "Ow ouch! Ow ouch! Ow ouch!"

(p. 10, Up, Up, Down)

So Tina got in the boat and rowed slow splash splash splash and the boat went in slow circles swish! swish! swish!

(p. 6, Smelly Socks)

Louis went into Andrew's house and got a pepper shaker. Then he pushed back Andrew's head and sprinkled pepper up Andrew's nose. Andrew went, "Ah, ah, ah, ah, ah-choo!"

(p. 24, Andrew's Loose Tooth)

When they got home, Lauretta put the wheelchair in first gear and rode up and down the driveway: zoom. But first gear was very slow. So she put it in tenth gear and went: zoom. That was still too slow, so she put it into twentieth gear and went really fast: zoom.

(p. 14, Zoom!)

So he got himself a piece of red play clay and whapped it in his hands — whap, whap, whap, whap, whap. Made it nice and round — swish, swish, swish, swish, swish. Sprinkled it with sugar — chik, chik, chik, chik, chik. Covered it with yellow icing — glick, glick, glick, glick, glick. And put some raisins on top — plunk, plunk, plunk, plunk, plunk.

(p. 4, Mmm, Cookies!)

He went up to a house: knock knock knock. A big man opened the door and said, "First kid for Halloween! So nice to see a little kid for Halloween." Lance lifted up his pillowcase and said, "Boo!" The man yelled, "Ah!" and fell right over.

(p. 8, Boo!)

Ideas for Munsch Author Study

- Write and perform a Readers' Theatre production of your favourite Munsch book. Note: *Andrew's Loose Tooth* works well.

- Make a puppet show with your favourite Munsch book.

- Design a book jacket for your favourite Robert Munsch book. The jackets could be laminated and displayed in a Munsch Corner in the classroom.

- Create a bookmark representing your favourite Munsch book. Choose a shape that reflects a character, building, or object in the book.

- Make character sketches for major characters in the Munsch books. What qualities do many of the main characters have in common?

- Use a shoebox or cardboard box to create a diorama of a scene from your favourite Robert Munsch book. Write a brief description about the book it came from, and which scene it represents. The dioramas and descriptions could be displayed in a glass case in the school.

- Create a Story Wheel of your favourite Robert Munsch book. Divide a circle into six to eight segments. Retell events of the story by moving clockwise around the circle.

- Make a Munsch Monument. Build a 3-D tribute to Munsch and include objects to represent the people or situations in his books. Explain what you included and why.

- Work with a partner to plan and create a mural of your favourite Robert Munsch book. The mural could centre on the events of a particular Robert Munsch book, or it could be a mural representing your favourite Munsch characters. Use a variety of media to create your mural. For example: paints, chalk, pastels, construction paper, cotton balls, chenille stems, coloured tissue, scraps of material.

- Have a special lunch and come as your favourite Munsch character. Call it A Meal for Munschkins. Remember to have cookies and pies for dessert!

- Write a story in the style of Robert Munsch. (Check Robert Munsch's website for some examples from other classes). Remember to include your favourite sound effects.

- Write a letter to Robert Munsch applying for a job as his assistant. Tell him why you would be a great candidate to help him do his job.

- Many of Munsch's stories are outlandish or crazy. Create your own crazy stories by brainstorming possible characters (names of people, animals, aliens), settings (the zoo, barnyard, home), and problems (running out of food, making too much noise) for stories. Have students write each character, setting, and problem idea they come up with on a separate slip of paper. Collect all the slips in three bags marked "Characters," "Setting," and "Problem." Pairs of students can then choose several slips from the character bag, one from the setting bag, and one from the problem bag. Ask them to work together to write a story using the characters and setting they drew, and resolving the problem they chose.

- Compare and contrast the zany Munsch books with his more serious books, like *Love You Forever, From Far Away,* and *Lighthouse.*

- Listen to some of the stories on Robert Munsch's website. Are the stories he tells exactly the same as the stories in the books? Why or why not? What makes Robert Munsch such an effective storyteller? Practise retelling your favourite Munsch story.

- Many children and school classes write to Robert Munsch and try to convince him to come and visit. Look at some of the examples on his website, and then write your own letters and invitations trying to convince Robert Munsch to come visit your school.

- Make a commercial for a Munsch book.

- Write newspaper reviews of your favourite Munsch stories.

- After reading and responding to many Munsch books, ask students to consider why so many children enjoy Robert Munsch's stories. What do they expect when they prepare to listen to a Munsch story?

- Compare the books with some of the videos that have been made of Robert Munsch's stories.

- Invite parents or another class to a Munsch celebration. Children can read their favourite Munsch stories to parents or younger students, or tell their favourite stories aloud.

- A class at Denne Elementary School in Newmarket, Ontario, got dressed up and held their own class awards show. Have your class do the same, and give out Munschie Awards for:
  - Best Major Character
  - Best Animal Character
  - Funniest Story
  - Best Illustrations
  - Favourite Story

LIST OF RESOURCES

Books by Robert Munsch

50 Below Zero
Aaron's Hair
Alligator Baby
Andrew's Loose Tooth
Angela's Airplane
Boo!
Boy in the Drawer, The
Dark, The
David's Father
Fire Station, The
From Far Away
Get Me Another One
Get Out of Bed!
Giant
Good Families Don't
I Have to Go!
I'm So Embarrassed!
Jonathan Cleaned Up – Then He Heard a Sound
Lighthouse
Love You Forever
Makeup Mess
Millicent and the Wind
Mmm, Cookies!
Moira's Birthday
More Pies!
Mortimer
Mud Puddle
Munsch More!
Munschworks
Munschworks 2
Munschworks 3
Munschworks 4
Munschworks Grand Treasury, The
Murmel, Murmel, Murmel
Paper Bag Princess, The
Pigs
Playhouse
Promise Is a Promise, A
Purple, Green and Yellow
Ribbon Rescue
Sandcastle Contest, The
Show and Tell
Smelly Socks
Something Good
Stephanie's Ponytail
Thomas' Snowsuit
Up, Up, Down
Wait and See
We Share Everything!
Where Is Gah-Ning?
Zoom!

Related Books

Andrew's Loose Tooth
Beeler, Selby B. (1998). *Throw Your Tooth on the Roof: Tooth Traditions from Around the World*
Copeland, Cynthia L. (2002). *The Tooth Fairy Tells All*
Edwards, Pamela Duncan. (2003). *Dear Tooth Fairy*
Hobbie, Holly. (2003). *Toot & Puddle: Charming Opal*
Luppens, Michael and Beha, Philippe. (1991). *What Do the Fairies Do With All Those Teeth?*
McPhail, David. (1978). *The Bear's Toothache*
Middleton, Charlotte. (2000). *Tabitha's Terrifically Tough Tooth*
Moss, Miriam. (2001). *Wibble Wobble*
O'Connor, Jane. (2002). *Dear Tooth Fairy*
Steig, William. (1982). *Doctor De Soto*

Mmm, Cookies!
Edwards, Nancy. (2001). *Glenna's Seeds*
Hooper, Meredith. (1997). *A Cow, a Bee, a Cookie, and Me*
Lamstein, Sarah. (1999). *I Like Your Buttons*
Murphy, Mary. (2002). *How Kind*

Smelly Socks
Donaldson, Chelsea. (2005). *Canada's Arctic Animals*
Harvey, Bev. (2004). *The Bear Family*
Hodge, Deborah. Wildlife Series *(Bears: Polar Bears, Black Bears, Grizzly Bears; Beavers; Deer, Moose, Elk and Caribou)*
McDermott, Barb. (1998). *All About Canadian Animals Series* (14 vols.)
Rue, Leonard Lee. (2002). *Beavers*

Up, Up, Down
Dorros, Arthur. (2002). *A Tree Is Growing*
Gibbons, Gail. (2002). *Tell Me, Tree: All About Trees for Kids*
Hoffman, Mary. (1991). *Amazing Grace*
Lauber, Patricia. (1994). *Be a Friend to Trees*
Locker, Thomas. (1995). *Sky Tree: Seeing Science Through Art*
McCully, Emily Arnold. (1992). *Mirette on the High Wire*
Mellett, Peter. (1997). *Learn About Trees*
Miller, Debbie S. (2002). *Are Trees Alive?*
Oppenheim, Joanne. (1995). *Have You Seen Trees?*
Pearson, Debora. (2004). *Leo's Tree*
Pinkney, J. Brian. (1998). *JoJo's Flying Side Kick*
Romanova, Natalia. (1985). *Once There Was a Tree*
Silverstein, Shel. (1964). *The Giving Tree*
Singh, Rina. (2003). *A Forest of Stories: Magical Tree Tales from Around the World*
Van Laan, Nancy. (2000). *A Tree for Me*
Wallace, Ian. (1984). *Chin Chiang and the Dragon's Dance*

Zoom!
Borba, Michele. (2001). *Building Moral Intelligence*
Carlson, Nancy. (1992). *Arnie and the New Kid*
Emmons, Chip. (2002). *Sammy Wakes His Dad*
Heelan, Jamee Riggio. (2000). *Rolling Along: the Story of Taylor and His Wheelchair*
Keith, Lois. (1999). *Being in a Wheelchair*
Lester, Helen. (1999). *Hooway for Wodney Wat!*
Lollis, Sylvia, et al. (2003). *Should We Have Pets? A Persuasive Text*
Pulver, Robin. (1999). *Way to Go, Alex!*
Schaefer, Lola M. (2001). *Some Kids Use Wheelchairs*

General Activity
Edwards, Pamela Duncan. (2001). *Slop Goes the Soup: A Noisy Warthog Word Book*
McDonald, Ross. (2003). *Achoo! Bang! Crash! A Noisy Alphabet*
Meister, Cari. (2000). *Busy, Busy City Street*
Rosen, Michael. (1993). *We're Going on a Bear Hunt*

Sayre, April Pulley. (2001). *It's My City: A Singing Map*
Spier, Peter. (1990). *Crash! Bang! Boom! A Book of Sounds*
Zelinsky, Paul O. (1990). *The Wheels on the Bus*

Websites

http://www.robertmunsch.com
The author's official web site.

http://www.scholastic.ca
Check Scholastic Canada's website for more information on Robert Munsch.

Videos

"The Life and Times of Robert Munsch" (2000) is an episode of CBC television's Life and Times series. It is designed for an adult audience but offers interesting insights into and information about Munsch's life and work. To order, see the CBC website at http://www.cbc.ca

"Meet the Author: Robert Munsch" (1985) is a short video from Mead Educational designed for a children's audience, with information about Munsch's life and work. It is available at most public libraries.

Book and Audio

"Tell Me a Story" Robert Munsch book-and-CD or book-and-cassette packages.

CD

Love You Forever: The Best of Robert Munsch (2003).

Additional Notes